Counseling?

....

When and Where to Get Help

Robert D. Jones

New
Growth
Press

newgrowthpress.com

New Growth Press, Greensboro, NC 27401
Copyright © 2022 by Robert D. Jones

Unless otherwise noted, Scripture quotations are taken from
the Holy Bible, New International Version®, NIV® Copyright
©1973, 1978, 1984, 2011 by Biblica, Inc.® Used by permission.
All rights reserved worldwide.

Cover Design: Dan Stelzer
Interior Typesetting and eBook: Gretchen Logterman

ISBN: 978-1-64507-212-6 (Print)
ISBN: 978-1-64507-213-3 (eBook)

Library of Congress Cataloging-in-Publication Data on File

Printed in India

29 28 27 26 25 24 23 22   1 2 3 4 5

Do you need counseling? The answer depends on what you mean by "counseling," and the kind of problem(s) you struggle with.

Are your personal or relational problems overwhelming you, negatively impacting your daily life or relationships? While all of us face the common pressures of living in a fallen world, sometimes those challenges become too much to handle alone and hinder us from effectively functioning the way God designed.

Perhaps you find yourself unable or temporarily unwilling to hear, believe, and apply God's counsel so that you can handle your problems on your own. Or it could be that your normal avenues of informal one-another care from your church seem insufficient, and you need a trained counselor to help you. These are times when you could benefit from focused help.

What kinds of problems might you address with a counselor? Perhaps you struggle with personal and internal problems like:

- Worry, fear, anxiety, or panic attacks
- Anger, bitterness, and resentment
- Doubts about your salvation and/or questions about God's goodness
- Bad habits, addictions, or chronic sinful patterns
- Sexual lust, masturbation, or fantasizing about others
- Sadness, disappointment, depression, or hopelessness

- Grief, bereavement, or other kinds of losses
- Self-harm or suicidal thoughts
- Eating disorders

Such problems can rob your inner peace, distract your mind, and consume you.

Or perhaps your struggle is interpersonal and relational—involving wrongs done *to* you by others, wrongs done *by* you to others, or both. Maybe you hurt someone or someone hurt you, and now feelings of distance or discomfort disrupt your relationship with your family member, friend, coworker, or fellow church member. In particular, marriage, parent-child, or extended family conflicts frequently need specific forms of relationship counseling.

Some problems might come from difficulties in handling suffering from general life hardships, such as natural disasters; economic downturns; accidents; or physical illness, disease, or disability. Or maybe you are suffering the impact of severe mistreatment or various forms of abuse, especially those resulting in trauma.

Do the problems you face involve present circumstances that need your immediate response, but you don't know what to do? Perhaps they involve unresolved past circumstances that presently invade your memories. What you did, what others did to you, or what happened to you currently haunts you.

Sometimes your problems might produce physical symptoms: high blood pressure, anxiety, sleeplessness, lethargy, gastrointestinal ailments, or no desire to eat. Those bodily symptoms, in turn, can affect your inner thoughts and feelings.

The presence of any of these factors suggests the need for formal counseling. In fact, maybe your specific struggle combines many of the above ingredients: personal and interpersonal, past and present, with and without physical manifestations. A counselor can help you sort out the issues as well as help you handle them.

Less Obvious Cases

Sometimes the need for counseling seems less apparent. Alyssa questions whether she needs counseling. In her two years of post-college ministry in a south Asian country, she experienced the ravages of poverty and conflict. She learned a lot about the world and the work being done there to help others, and she also learned about herself. She came back to the U.S. and has had a hard time adjusting to the affluence of her parents' suburban neighborhood. Things that never bothered her before now stir feelings of anger, bitterness, or guilt. She wonders how to handle her discomfort and what to do with her life.

As Tyler contemplated his own struggle, he asked himself the same question. A twenty-nine-year-old single man, he lives in the apartment above his parents' garage and has no social life. He attends the church he grew up in, but the community has changed in recent years and he doesn't connect well with the new pastor or many of the older congregants. His best friend Brandon is married with two children; Tyler hangs out with them every few weeks, but that's about the extent of his friendships. His mom and dad and Brandon all say he needs a wife, but he hasn't been on a date in more than three years. He is not opposed to the idea—he just doesn't know how to proceed.

Early on, God used marriage counseling to save Derek and Chloe's marriage. Now, fifteen years later, they are enjoying their life. However, Chloe's mom was recently diagnosed with multiple sclerosis, and Chloe's sister who lives near their mom is the primary caretaker. Chloe thinks they should visit their parents more often and share the load with her sister, but Derek loves teaching his Sunday School class and doesn't like to travel on weekends. They too wonder if they need counseling.

Thankfully, each person answered yes to this question. They met with a caring biblical counselor and found God's help through God's Spirit working through the application of God's Word.

If you aren't sure if you need counseling, ask a trusted friend, relative, mentor, and/or pastor. Someone who knows you well can usually help you decide if you should seek formal counseling.

What Type of Counseling Do I Need?

Assuming you decide formal counseling will help you, what kind should you seek? This minibook proposes an approach called biblical counseling. Before unpacking the nature of formal biblical counseling, let's consider the need every person has for God's Word and the various ways we might receive that general help.

In one sense, everyone needs the counsel from God's Word to live the way God designed. In fact, even before sin entered the world, our ancestors Adam and Eve needed God's counsel to help them understand their identity as his image-bearers and to fulfill his purposes for them. They listened to and enjoyed God's voice—the one voice, the voice of truth (Genesis 1–2).

Then, at one fatal point, Satan appeared. Adam and Eve listened to his voice—the voice of evil and a false counselor. When they listened to Satan instead of their heavenly Father, they became alienated from God and one another. Yet God did not abandon them. He continued to speak to them, teaching them how to get right with him, how to live to please him, and how to navigate the hardships and effects of the fall. God mercifully covered their nakedness and promised them a Redeemer who would come through their lineage (Genesis 3:15).

Since then, the competition between God's pure voice of love and the ungodly voices of the world, the flesh, and the devil have continued (Genesis 4–Revelation 19) and will continue until God silences their voices forever in final judgment (Revelation 20) and brings his people into his new heaven and earth (Revelation 21–22). On that day, those who belong to him will hear his "loud voice from the throne saying, 'Look! God's dwelling place is now among the people, and he will dwell with them. They will be his people, and God himself will be with them and be their God. . . . 'I am making everything new!'" (Revelation 21:3, 5).

Different Kinds of Biblical Help

Believers in Christ can be shaped by biblical truth in various ways. First, we hear his voice revealed in his Word through our personal Bible reading. We can call this *self-counseling*: the private, prayerful study, reflection, and application of Scripture to our own lives. This is a foundational practice for healthy growth and flourishing in the Christian life.

Moreover, we also need the *informal counseling* Christians give each other. God uses his people—pastors and fellow church members—to help us grasp and live out the counsel of his Word. This includes preaching and teaching, along with one-on-one Bible reading and group Bible study. Healthy churches provide a familial setting where we can receive biblically consistent counsel from each other.

However, beyond these forms of Bible intake, sometimes we need more *formal counseling*: regular, structured meetings with a trained biblical counselor to address one or more specific problems that we and our counselor have together identified.

What Is Formal Biblical Counseling?

Thankfully, in the past fifty years, a new and growing form of Christian counseling has reemerged: biblical counseling, "the Christlike, caring, person-to-person ministry of God's Word to people struggling with personal and interpersonal problems to help them know and follow Jesus Christ in heart and behavior amid their struggles."[1]

Let's consider six key concepts biblical counselors typically prioritize.[2] These elements are the core building blocks for a counselor's approach to your problems. You will want to ask questions to know where your counselor's advice will come from.

1. ***Scripture.*** Biblical counseling is not just counseling done by a therapist who is a Christian, quotes the Bible, or uses Scripture as an occasional supplement.

Rather, in biblical counseling, Scripture drives the actual content and methodology of the counseling session. The Bible doesn't merely *inform* our theory and practice; it *forms* what we think and do. It is not just one truth source among many; it's the truth (John 17:17) that propels our approach and controls how we look at God, ourselves, other people, our problems, and the change process.

This means that biblical counselors use the Bible to diagnose, explain, and solve counseling problems. As God's Word, it provides true, thorough, authoritative, and sufficient guidance for each life situation people face, and it is richly superior to human wisdom and competing forms of therapy. The Bible provides precisely what every counselee deeply needs: it refreshes the soul, makes people wise, and gives "joy to the heart" and "light to the eyes" (Psalm 19:7–8). We build our counseling on the apostle Paul's conviction, "All Scripture is God-breathed and is useful for teaching, rebuking, correcting and training in righteousness, so that the servant of God may be thoroughly equipped for every good work" (2 Timothy 3:16–17).

2. ***Jesus Christ.*** Biblical counselors present the Lord Jesus as the crucified, risen, reigning, and returning Savior who, through his Word and his Spirit, helps people handle their personal and relational problems. Christ is "the one we proclaim, admonishing and teaching everyone with all wisdom, so that we may present everyone fully mature in Christ" (Colossians 1:28). He can "empathize with our weaknesses," as one "who has been tempted in every way, just as we

are—yet he did not sin," and the one from whom Christians "may receive mercy and find grace to help us in our time of need" (Hebrews 4:15–16).

Biblical counselors lead their counselees to rely on a Redeemer outside of themselves to come *to* them and come *into* them by his Spirit to change them. No other form of therapy will accomplish God's good agenda for them.

3. ***The Holy Spirit.*** Biblical counselors recognize God's Spirit as the one who wrote the Bible and as the Redeemer's indwelling agent in the lives of those we counsel. We depend on the Holy Spirit to give us his wisdom and power to carry out our ministry and to bring about needed change in our counselees. Christ's Spirit increasingly transforms believers into Christ's image (2 Corinthians 3:18), empowers them to know Christ better (Ephesians 3:16–17), and produces in them growing Christian maturity (Romans 8:11–14). We fill the counseling process with prayer and urge counselees to do the same.

4. ***Heart and Behavior.*** Because biblical counselors believe God's Spirit seeks thorough and lasting godly change in those we counsel, we address both heart and behavior—both the inward and outward issues of a person's problems. Biblical counselors believe all behavior "flows" from the heart (Proverbs 4:23), all speech emerges from "what the heart is full of" (Matthew 12:34), and "out of the heart come evil thoughts—murder, adultery, sexual immorality, theft, false testimony, slander" (Matthew 15:19). Moreover, we are confident that "the word of God is alive and active. . . . [I]t judges the thoughts and

attitudes of the heart" (Hebrews 4:12). Scripture alone uncovers and solves our inner heart struggles—our core beliefs, motives, desires, affections—and our outer behavioral struggles.

5. **Compassion.** Aided by the Holy Spirit, biblical counselors seek to reflect the love, concern, and compassion of Jesus our Shepherd and Counselor, who, "when he saw the crowds, he had compassion on them, because they were harassed and helpless, like sheep without a shepherd" (Matthew 9:36). Biblical counseling is a caring process marked by Christlike love (1 Corinthians 13:4–8), the fruit of his Spirit (Galatians 5:22–23), and "compassion, kindness, humility, gentleness and patience" (Colossians 3:12). We recognize that counseling problems often entail various forms and degrees of suffering. Christlike compassion extends to those who suffer not only from the sins of others but also from the consequences of their own sins (e.g., Nehemiah 9:16–21).

6. **The Church.** Biblical counselors value healthy, Bible-believing churches, and we view their pastors and members as God's primary ministers of grace for those we counsel. Even biblical counselors who counsel in parachurch, meta-church, or state-licensed settings stress the primacy and centrality of God's church in helping people change (1 Timothy 3:14–15). Biblical counselors point counselees to their local church for continual support, nurture, and service opportunities. We share Paul's confidence, "I myself am convinced, my brothers and sisters, that you yourselves are full of goodness, filled with knowledge and competent to instruct one

another" (Romans 15:14; cf. Colossians 3:16). We also share Paul's vision, "speaking the truth in love, we will grow to become in every respect the mature body of him who is the head, that is, Christ. From him the whole body, joined and held together by every supporting ligament, grows and builds itself up in love, as each part does its work" (Ephesians 4:15–16).

While these six priorities should mark biblical counselors, too often we fall short of these standards. We are far from perfect. The apostle James reminds us, "We all stumble in many ways" (James 3:2). (Yet, hopefully, when we do, we seek to make things right with God and with those we counsel.) Moreover, biblical counselors vary in their knowledge and ability. As in any people-helping ministry or profession, any individual biblical counselor might have more or less training, experience, and relational skill than another biblical counselor. Nevertheless, these six priorities lie at the heart of what biblical counselors believe and seek to practice.

Practical Questions
Where might I find a biblical counselor?
As already mentioned, your fellow church members can and should provide informal counseling as you minister to one another. Often that mutual care can sufficiently help you and preempt the need for formal counseling. However, sometimes we need formal biblical counseling, the kind done in scheduled sessions by a counselor with a higher level of training from a Bible college, seminary, or biblical counseling training organization. That trained counselor might be a church pastor

or elder or some other vocational minister (e.g., missionary, church planter, campus minister, men's or women's ministry director, student minister). Or the counseling might be provided by trained lay members: men and women designated or certified as biblical counselors in their church or parachurch organization. Many churches train their members to counsel each other and sometimes those in the community seeking help. In other cases, the counselor might be a state-licensed counselor who counsels people biblically and is able to work within the ethical parameters of their secular state license.

If you desire counseling, start with your pastor. Briefly summarize your struggle and ask him if he or another elder can provide biblical counseling (as described above) or recommend someone in the church. (Just today, my lead pastor referred a couple to me for marriage counseling—the beauty of the local church at work.) Or you might start with your small group leader(s) to see if they can provide that help or recommend someone in the church. Perhaps your church already has a procedure in place where you can approach an approved counselor.

If your church doesn't provide biblical counseling, your pastor might refer you to someone outside the church. You can also search biblical counseling websites that list or recommend counselors or parachurch ministries.[3] While in-person counseling is preferable, some biblical counselors provide virtual counseling for those in more remote locations. If that search is unsuccessful, you might contact local Bible-believing churches to see if they provide biblical counseling for nonmembers or recommend other options.

Finally, just as you would assess any physician or professional before seeking their help, evaluate potential biblical counselors. Consider questions like these:

- Does the counselor value the six biblical counseling priorities above? For example, are they themselves active members in a healthy, Bible-believing church? Do they regularly use their Bible in counseling sessions?
- What general education (e.g., a bachelor's, master's, or doctoral degree) and what specific biblical counseling training have they completed? Did their training include practicum components in which they observed an experienced biblical counselor or were observed and supervised by an experienced counselor? What certifications, if any, do they have?
- Are they part of a church or organization? If so, what do you know about the church or organization? Or are they counseling in private practice? If so, why?
- How clearly do they explain confidentiality, financial costs, the length and frequency of sessions, the freedom to bring a friend, communicating with your church, and other procedural matters? Are you comfortable and confident in their ability to help you?

In some cases, you might consider a brief interview before committing to a session.

What about counsel related to problematic psychiatric disorders?

Perhaps your counseling struggle is unusually severe, involving severe mood or cognitive problems—e.g., debilitating depression, audible hallucinations, manic episodes, or panic attacks. Maybe you have been diagnosed with some psychiatric disorder by a state-licensed therapist.

Biblical counselors can certainly play a valuable role even, or especially, in these cases. First, we can remind you that God your Creator and Provider knows you intimately and cares for you deeply (Psalm 103:13–18). His Spirit understands the depths of even your most troubling thoughts and confused desires (Psalm 139:1–6, 23–24; Romans 7:14–25; 8:26–27). In fact, he knows you better than you know yourself and he invites you to cry out to him for help.

Second, because biblical counselors care about your body and not just your soul, we recognize that various physical factors (e.g., neurological or endocrine problems) can interfere with someone's daily functioning. In such cases, we routinely recommend counselees go to a medical doctor for a full physical examination to diagnose or rule out medical maladies.

Third, all psychiatric problems have a spiritual dimension, since humans exist in unity of two interrelated substances: material (physical body) and immaterial (heart, spirit, soul, or mind). Whether or not some pathology is medically discovered or merely theorized, and whether or not the person begins a psychotropic medication,[4] biblical counselors can bring clarity, hope, and encouragement through God's Word to those facing such suffering (Hebrews 4:12; Proverbs 20:5).

Fourth, as I have seen in my counseling ministry, you might find that some of these complex issues prove to be more spiritual and internal than you realized. Biblical counseling might help decrease the troubling symptoms and grow your sense of peace, joy, and stability in Christ.

Is biblical counseling confidential?

We assume you want a counselor who is not only Christlike, competent, and caring, but also a counselor who won't divulge your personal information to others. For this reason, biblical counselors regard confidentiality as a necessary component in the counseling process. Scripture prohibits gossip and prioritizes privacy and relational trust, e.g., Proverbs 11:13, "A gossip betrays a confidence, but a trustworthy man keeps a secret" (see also 17:9; 20:19). Our Lord's words add a further reason to maintain confidentiality: "So in everything, do to others what you would have them do to you, for this sums up the Law and the Prophets" (Matthew 7:12). If I want you to guard my private information, I should guard yours. I tell those I counsel, "What we discuss stays between us."

At same time, biblical counselors don't guarantee absolute confidentiality. Like other helping professions, we practice limited confidentiality. At times—albeit rarely in my experience—a biblical counselor might need to disclose otherwise private information to appropriate other people, such as civil or church authorities (Romans 13:1–5; Hebrews 13:17), if he or she thinks you or someone else might be in danger of harm or if he or she suspects abuse or neglect of minors or the elderly. Your counselor can explain to you his or her confidentiality commitments. You should clarify these matters before you proceed with counseling.

At the same time, since formal counseling is typically a voluntary commitment, most biblical counselors free both the counselee and counselor to discontinue the process at any time without explanation. On your end, you might find that you and your counselor don't seem to click relationally, that you disagree on a significant point of Bible interpretation or application, or that you doubt your counselor's Christlikeness, competency, care, or confidentiality.

Is there a financial cost?

If your church provides biblical counseling, those counselors normally don't charge a fee or expect a financial contribution from members, except perhaps to purchase any assigned reading or study materials as part of the counseling process. Paid staff pastors or counselors provide members free counseling as part of their ministry. Lay pastors or counselors volunteer their time without financial remuneration to serve their church family. (Of course, if you appreciate their ministry, you might give him or her a gift card or make a special contribution to the church's counseling fund.)

If you seek biblical counseling from a parachurch center or private counselor, plan to pay a professional fee. If you seek it from another church, consider a per-session donation to allow that church to provide this ministry to nonmembers like you.

What might I experience in a session?

While each biblical counselor has his or her own unique procedures and techniques, most follow a similar pattern. Before the first session, your counselor will likely ask you to review or complete several forms: a brief overview of the problem, a detailed personal information form, and an agreement form that explains confidentiality and seeks your informed consent to be counseled. You might be asked to email or upload those documents before the first session or bring them when you meet.

In the first session, you can expect to be greeted warmly and treated respectfully. Your counselor will introduce him or herself, along with any co-counselor, assistant, or trainee who might be present. Your counselor will invite you to share your background and your current struggles, and will carefully listen and caringly ask questions to gain needful information. He or she will seek to understand you and make sure you feel understood.

At some point, usually in the first session but at least by the second session, your counselor will bring you a biblical perspective about your problem and give you relevant Scripture to help you think about that problem and apply God's Word to your life and situation. In addition, your counselor typically will give you something to do after the session, a reasonable growth assignment to help you further apply biblical truth from this session and prepare you for the next. Moreover, your counselor will encourage you to seek support, encouragement, and accountability within your local church, or help you find a healthy one. Finally, your counselor will pray for you and offer to meet with you again to continue the process

Again, biblical counselors vary in their individual style. And of course, no counselor is perfect. But most biblical counselors, especially those approved by their church, serving with a reputable biblical counseling center, or certified by a biblical counseling certifying organization (see endnote 3) will meet those standards and can bring you Christ's help from God's Word.

How can I make the process most beneficial?

If you decide to meet with a biblical counselor, six commitments can help you increase the effectiveness of the counseling process.

1. Be committed to *biblical* counseling. Be eager to hear, believe, and do God's Word. Come to each session with a humble, teachable spirit, seeking to learn how God wants you to handle your life based on Scripture. Pray beforehand. Bring your Bible and a notepad to help you retain the counseling insights during the session and apply them afterward.
2. Be as open and honest as you can. Though talking about your problems might be difficult for you and developing trust in your counselor might take time, your transparency—combined with your growing trust in God—can accelerate the growth process.
3. Be patient—your problems did not develop in a day. It may take your counselor several sessions to get to know you and understand your

situation. Wise counselors listen carefully and gather thorough information. Only foolish counselors give quick answers to complex situations (Proverbs 18:13; 20:5).

4. Between sessions, complete the growth assignments given, and review and pray over the matters discussed during previous sessions. For most biblical counselors, such assignments are an integral part of the process, as important as the session itself. It's during the 167 hours between weekly sessions that God typically brings about the most change. View the session like a piano lesson: the teacher corrects your bad habits and teaches you new skills, but you only learn to play by practicing the techniques you learned in the lesson.

5. Consider the possibility of inviting a godly, mature friend or mentor to join you in the sessions, or at least to pray for you and hear what you are learning in the sessions. Most biblical counselors encourage this. That person might be a trusted Christian friend, a fellow church member, a pastor (or their spouse), a small group leader (or their spouse), or your spouse if you are married. Before the session, that person can encourage you to come and help you prepare. During the session, your friend can help you understand and remember the counsel given. After the session, he or she can provide you with support, encouragement, and accountability.

6. Along with personal spiritual disciplines like Bible reading and prayer, participate regularly

and actively in the life and ministry of your local church. Regular participation in a Christ-centered, biblical church provides you with vital complements to biblical counseling: God-centered worship that lifts your eyes to the attributes and acts of our triune God, sound Bible teaching with practical life application, pastoral care, and meaningful small group life and other relationships with sisters and brothers who are also learning and displaying God's grace to each other.

My Prayer for You

Here's what I hope this minibook will help you find, prioritize, and enjoy:

You will meet with someone who will welcome you warmly, listen to you carefully, empathize with you compassionately, and speak to you wisely. Your counselor will set before you the way of life found in Jesus Christ and all of Christ's provisions for you. In handling Scripture, he or she will select timely passages that connect to your life, explain them clearly, and help you apply them practically. Your counselor will know when to push you and when to support you, when to "comfort the afflicted" or "afflict the comfortable."

In all this, your counselor will depend on God's Spirit to change you, will pray *with* you and *for* you, and will help you connect well to your local church (pastors, small group leaders, fellow members) or find a healthy church. He or she will work with you for the season needed, will recognize limits, will envision and plan for the day you will graduate from formal counseling, and will realize that some problems will not be fully resolved until Christ returns and you enjoy an eternity with him in the new heaven and earth.

Here is my prayer for you: that you would understand the love God has for you, and that as you seek biblical counseling help for your problems, whether personal or relational, whether severe or less so, that the heavenly Father in his mercy will draw you near to himself and bring you hope and help. I'm praying the Lord will bring you the truths you need from his Word, that you would know Jesus either for the first time or in a deeper way. I'm praying he would lead you to a biblical counselor and a local church that will bring you his life-giving grace and truth.

Endnotes

1. Robert D. Jones, "What Is Biblical Counseling?" in Robert D. Jones, Kristin L. Kellen, and Rob Green, *The Gospel for Disordered Lives: An Introduction to Christ-Centered Biblical Counseling* (Nashville: B&H Academic, 2021), 20. For a more thorough description of biblical counseling, see the Confessional Statement of the Biblical Counseling Coalition, https://www.biblicalcounselingcoalition.org/confessional-statement.

2. Adapted from Jones, "What Is Biblical Counseling?" 12–19. Reused with permission.

3. Examples of certifying organizations include the Association of Certified Biblical Counselors, the Association of Biblical Counselors, and the International Association of Biblical Counselors. The Biblical Counseling Coalition's website lists groups like these and other referral options: https://partners.biblicalcc.org/counselor-map/.

4. For concise, helpful insight on these matters, see Michael R. Emlet, *Descriptions and Prescriptions: A Biblical Perspective on Psychiatric Diagnoses and Medications* (Greensboro, NC: New Growth Press, 2017).

Simple, Quick, Biblical

Advice on Complicated Counseling Issues
for Pastors, Counselors, and Individuals

MINIBOOK
CATEGORIES

- Personal Change
- Marriage & Parenting
- Medical & Psychiatric Issues
- Women's Issues
- Singles
- Military